Nature Walks.

Joys of Walking.

Mohinder Pal Singh

BookLeaf
Publishing

India | USA | UK

Made with ❤ on the BookLeaf Publishing Platform
www.bookleafpub.in
www.bookleafpub.com

Dedication

This book of poems is dedicated to my wife Arvinder, and to my family, who have stood by me through thick & thin.

Preface

A Walk a Day keeps the Doctor away.

A Walk is the best way to begin the day, and no better way to end the day, than to walk as the evening shadows lengthen.

Walking brings health benefits and clears the mental cobwebs.

Walking is therapeutic and does not need physical training and equipment.

Best of all, walking is Free, non polluting and sustainable, in a world centred around material consumption.

Acknowledgements

Every journey starts with the first steps. My wife
Arvinder, literally drew me out of slumber and a lazy
lifestyle , and goaded me to shake a leg, and to take the
first steps.
Once the walking bug bit me, there was no turning back.
One step led to another, and soon, I was addicted to daily
walks.
There was no turning back, after that.

1. Why I walk .

The Joys of Walking ,
in Nature,
by the Lakes and Bubbling Brooks,
Calm my soul,
And give me Solace,
That satisfies my Spirit.

I walk because I must
Else I rust.
Walks are the soul's medicine,
More than physical fitness.

Soothing and uplifting,
Walks bring cheer,
and Peace that Endures.

2. Walk don't Run.

Leave the rat race for rats,
Take the Slow Lane,
Savor Life,
Let others race past,
My Pace is Mine.

A Leisurely Walk,
Brings Pleasure.

Leisure without Pleasure,
is Tiring,
Pleasure without Purpose,
is Pointless.

Let us go,
into the garden,
into the pathways,
to a new world.

Open our soul eyes,
for the first time.

3. Bird Song.

Birds singing in the trees,
A Sweet Song,
A sweet rhapsody,
Wafting gently,
in the evening breeze.

Birds winging their way home,
Flying as one,
in a geometric formation,
Beauty in motion.

Birds silhouetted,
Against the evening sky,
Like a painter's ,
Brush strokes,
On the canvas of the sky.

4. Trees .

Trees spread out their canopies,
Dappled shadows in the sun,
Dancing in rhythm.

Leaves on a bough,
Take a bow,
As the sun arcs,
Across the firmament.

Leaves lazily drift down,
as if the day
Belongs to them.

Leaves silently
Cover the forest floor,
A steady pitter patter.

Rejoice not,
O man,
They too

will fade
into the dusk.

5. Forest.

A Forest ,
is Alive.
A Forest throbs,
with Life,
that is
Forever Changing,
with the Changing Seasons.

A Forest is Life
in a Myriad Forms,
Now Green,
Now Fallen,
Leaves to the Forest Floor.

Embrace Nature !
Embrace a Tree,
Embrace Life !

Feel the Forest Pulse,
Feel Deeply,

Breathe Deeply.
Feel the rhythm,
the Forest never sleeps.

6. The Tranquil Night.

The bees are busy doing
Best what the Lord GOD Made them for
Humming & Buzzing .

The Birds Perch Prettily on trees,
Evening is creeping upon them,
But the birds are chirping & cheeping,
Their hearts in Birdsongs.

Soon dusk throws it's mantle over the land,
And evening brings stillness and quiet.

Nature is never still,
Dogs take over,
Making their presence felt,
Faithful Sentinels of the night,
like a night watchman.

Night throws her cloak over the forest,
And finally quiet and peace breathes a sigh.

7. Evening Notes.

Slowly, ever so slowly,
The day winds down,
Like a clock that loses it's spring.

A hush descends on the lake,
The Shikara turns around,
The boats follow suit,
The merry makers reluctantly
fall in line,
Like truant children,
Brought to heel
By their minders
who shepherd them
Like sheep.

The splash of the oars
travels quietly over the water,
Over the silvery sheen.

The moon peeps

Shyly from the clouds,
Many a Majnu serenades
His Laila queen.

A cool breeze blows,
Sending couples cuddling
Ashore.

The Night reclaims it's
Rights over the
Remnants of the Day.

8. Go with God.

Go with God,
Go with Waheguru.

Nature is Pure
& Walking
Brings Joy,
A breath of Fresh Air
And a Mind that opens
To Daily Miracles.

Walk to the beat of your heart,
And watch Nature's
Creatures big and small.

Walk on the grass,
Walk off the beaten path,
Walk and walk,
Walk the Talk .

Be Renewed,

Be Refreshed,
Be Revived,
Rejuvenated,
And Reborn.

9. River .

By the River.

A River is never still,
Always in flow,
Like a person in slow rhythm
Dancing to a beat,
Only heard by him.

O River,
Teach me to flow
Quietly,
Smoothly.

So that I can flow on,
On and on.

Teach me to be mindful,
Of the beauty around me,
Of the flowers and the bees.

Fleeting beauty,
Ever changing,
Ever blooming.

10. Boats.

Boats.
Boats on the lake,
Creating ripples
Rippling outwards
Merging into waves
Murmuring with the wind.

Ripples that rock boats,
Ripples that reach the shores,
The oars dip and creak,
As the boats bob
And rise,
Rise and ride
The waves.

Time & Tide
Wait for no one,
Turn the boat
Around,
Into the current

That flows,
Like life
That ebbs
And flows.

11. God's Garden.

Walk with reverence
For all things,
Step with care
On all grasses.

Watch mindfully
Each flower,
Walk slowly,
Look carefully,
Yesterday's flowers
Are today's Nature's carpet.

Many have come & gone,
Leave no footprints ,
In God's Garden.

12. Collect Memories.

Like travellers,
We pass through,
Be a beggar in possessions,
Like a king in memories.

Not a collector of things,
But a collector of
Precious Moments.

The busy bee
Collects pollen from flowers,
The honey does not belong to the bee.

Go off the beaten tracks,
Meander into serendepitous
Moments,
Let nature reveal it's bounty.

13. Health is Wealth.

Health is the true wealth,
Walking is Non-polluting,
Non violent,
Eco balance friendly.

Health comes in the forefront.
Benefits many,
Why hesitate?

Walkers unite,
No loss,
All gains,
Hesitate not.

Procrastination the thief
That steals silently.
Let it not steal
Good health.

14. Walk Time.

Anytime to Walk
is a good Time.
Evening,
Morning,
Noon,
Dawn.

When dawn breaks,
All is silent,
Then birds awaken,
Take wing,
Early bird catches the worm.

The sun shines
Brightly at Noon,
The leaves play
Hide & Seek
In the trees
With sunlight.

The Heat is on !
Best to rest in the shade,
Even birds and bees
Seek the shade.

Water is the need
of the Noon Hour
A refreshing dip
For the feet in the lake.

The sun moves on,
The heat is cooler,
The sun rays
No longer
Fierce

Evening brings solace,
Relief and cool breeze.

Night falls,
All is still.

15. Heartfelt.

Gladdens my heart,
To sally forth
Into the grassy paths.

Grass may be Greener
On the other side,
But there is green
Grass everywhere
to gladden the heart.

The dew drops
Cling to the grass,
And catch the Sun Rays,
Glinting like pearls.

Gather the dew drops,
Before the sun
Captures them
Basking in the sun

16. Golf and Walking.

Golf is ideal for walking
and Playing a restful sport.
More than a game,
Golf soothes
and Rejuvenates.

Play 9 or 18 holes,
Golf sets it's own pace,
and never forces the pace.

A Hole in One,
An unexpected bonus,
Goes straight into
record books,
And memories.

Golf is a Golden Game,
paying dividends,
Unexpected Delights.

17. Walk slowly.

Walk slowly,
Savor Nature's Sights
And Sounds.

Walk with an open mind,
Receive Nature's Blessings,
Nature's Bounty.

Walk with an Attitude
Of Gratitude,
Be thankful
To God,
For giving the opportunity
To sample Nature's Delights.

Trust in Nature's Wisdom,
Trust God's Will,
Trust in God.

18. Believe in God.

God makes the world go around,
God made all the creatures
Big and small.

Seek God's Blessings
And you will be Blessed.

Walk to thank God,
Walk to count
Your Blessings.

Walk to open your eyes,
Walk to open your mind.

Nature knows no limits,
God's mercy
Falls on all.
Big and small.

19. Infinite Wonders.

Nature's Wonders never cease,
Infinite in Abundance

Feel the grass
Under your feet,
Connect to
A greater reality.

Spirit of Wonder,
Spirit of Humility,
Spirit of learning,
Attitude counts.

A walk teaches
Many Lessons,
Beauty that never
Fades,
Nature's Colors
Paint myriad hues.

20. Walking Plus.

Walk you way to Good Health,
Walk your way to a Happier Life .

Walking helps the mind to see
With New Eyes,
Like new spectacles.

Walking clears the mental fog,
The mental cobwebs.

Colors look more vivid,
Nature itself looks brighter,
As if washed by rain.

The mind Gains new insights,
New perspectives.

Beauty wears a new look,
The grass looks greener.

Breathe deep
Nature's Clean air,
Break free from pollution
And dust.

No cost,
No fees,
Nature is Free,
Unlimited
Unadulterated.

21. Rainbow

As I walk,
Clouds overcast the blue sky,
A light rain starts falling.

The gentle pitter patter of the rain,
Raindrops falling on my head,
Cool my brow.

I do not take cover,
And Let the rain
Clear my thoughts.

A light breeze
Springs up,
And Lo and Behold,
The clouds scatter,

The blue sky
Slowly shyly
Shows it's

True colors.

The sun peeps out,
Like a child
From behind his mother's apron.

A single ray of sunshine
Lifts my spirits.
Then the small miracle
And a splendid rainbow
Arches across the sky.

Nature surprises
With multi colored hues,
God is in Heaven,
And all is well
In this world.

.